The Gifts of
KWANZAA

Synthia Saint James

ALBERT WHITMAN & COMPANY
Morton Grove, Illinois

For Jessica, Ray, Janine, Michael,
Sacha, Chela, and Sancho.

Thanks to Limbiko Tembo and Chimbuko Tembo
of the University of Sankore Press.

Library of Congress Cataloging-in-Publication Data

Saint James, Synthia.
The gifts of Kwanzaa / written and illustrated by Synthia Saint James.
p.   cm.
ISBN 0-8075-2907-9
1. Kwanzaa—Juvenile literature. [1. Kwanzaa. 2. Afro-Americans—
Social life and customs.] I. Title.
GT4403.S25 1994   94-1168
394.2'61—dc20   CIP   AC

Designer: Susan B. Cohn
Text Type: Kabel Medium
Illustration medium: acrylic on canvas

ABOUT KWANZAA

In 1966, Dr. Maulana Karenga created the celebration known as *Kwanzaa* (KWAHN-zaah) for all people of African descent. It is intended to reaffirm our culture and values as well as the bonds that hold us together as a people.

"Kwanzaa," which means "first fruits" in the African language of Swahili, is celebrated for seven days, from December 26 to January 1. Swahili is the language used at Kwanzaa because it is spoken widely throughout Africa.

There are seven principles of Kwanzaa, one for each day. They were designed especially for our children, our future. *Habari gani* (hah-BAH-ree GAH-nee)—"What news?"—is the greeting used each morning. The answer is the name of the principle for that day. Seven candles—one black, three red, and three green—stand for the seven principles. Each night, one candle is lit, and the family talks about the principle for that day.

There are also seven symbols of Kwanzaa: a mat on which the other symbols rest; fruits and vegetables, representing the harvest; a unity cup, from which all drink; a candleholder with seven places; the seven candles themselves; an ear of corn for each child in the home; and gifts from the parents to the children.

Kwanzaa has become an important holiday. It is now celebrated by millions of people the world over—in the United States, Europe, Canada, the Caribbean, and parts of Africa.

*H*abari gani? What news?

It's Kwanzaa time! Kwanzaa time is here!

Mom carries in the *mkeka*
(em–KAY–kah),
the mat that we place
on our Kwanzaa table.
It's made of bright straw
and stands for our foundation.
I bring the *kikombe cha umoja*
(kee–KOM–bay chah oo–MOH–jah),
the unity cup.
We all drink from this cup,
for we are one people.

Now on the *mkeka*
we place symbols of the harvest—
fresh fruits and vegetables
called the *mazao* (mah-ZAH-o)
and ears of corn called *muhindi*
(moo-HEEN-dee).
This Kwanzaa, we have three ears—
one for each child in our family.

On the first day of Kwanzaa,
I light the one black candle
in the *kinara* (kee-NAH-rah),
the candleholder.
It shines for our pride
in the black race.
We light the red candle
the next day
to remember our struggle;
the green on the next
for our hopes and our dreams.
Then red, green, red, green,
until all seven are lit.

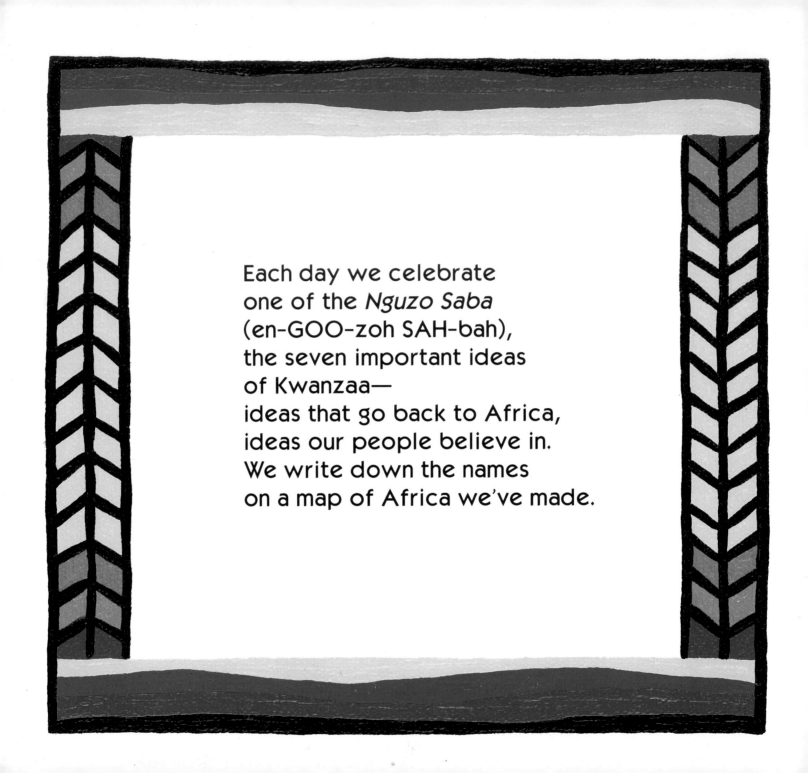

Each day we celebrate
one of the *Nguzo Saba*
(en-GOO-zoh SAH-bah),
the seven important ideas
of Kwanzaa—
ideas that go back to Africa,
ideas our people believe in.
We write down the names
on a map of Africa we've made.

UMOJA

KUJICHAGULIA

UJIMA

UJAMAA

NIA

KUUMBA

IMANI

First comes *Umoja*
(oo-MOH-jah).
This is for unity,
for sticking together
at work and at play,
in good times and bad.

Self-determination is next.
We call it *Kujichagulia*
(koo-jee-chah-goo-LEE-ah).
It's deciding for ourselves
what's right and what's wrong.
It's planning what we
will become,
and studying hard at school.

The third day, *Ujima* (oo-JEE-mah),
is for coming together to get things done right.

We help in our homes, we join with our neighbors,
to keep everything beautiful, to keep our lives good.

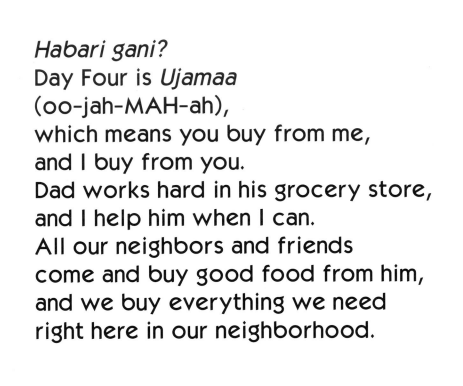

Habari gani?
Day Four is *Ujamaa*
(oo-jah-MAH-ah),
which means you buy from me,
and I buy from you.
Dad works hard in his grocery store,
and I help him when I can.
All our neighbors and friends
come and buy good food from him,
and we buy everything we need
right here in our neighborhood.

Purpose, or *Nia* (NEE-ah),
is for the fifth day.
We work to restore
the greatness of our people.
We learn of our leaders
and our proud history.
We dress like our
African ancestors
of long ago.

Being creative—
we call it *Kuumba*
(koo-OOM-bah)—
is the magic that comes
on Day Number Six.
My best friend makes up dances,
and Nana sews on the family quilt.
My brothers and I
paint the sun, sea, and sky
on the wall of Dad's store.

That night is the *karamu* (kah-RAH-moo), the feast
and the giving of gifts. Good friends come over,

we eat African food, and play happy African music.
We all learn a new dance—even my baby brother!

Mom and Dad give us *zawadi*
(zah-WAH-dee),
presents for promises
we've worked hard to keep.
There are gifts from Africa
like drums, dolls, and flutes,
and wonderful books
that tell about our past.

On the seventh and last day,
faith is the key.
Faith is *Imani* (ee-MAH-nee)—
it's belief in ourselves,
our families, and our culture.
We gather to light all seven candles,
the *mishumaa saba*
(mee-shoo-MAH-ah SAH-bah).
They glow bright for Kwanzaa—
they glow bright for our joy!

NGUZO SABA (en-GOO-zoh SAH-bah)
The Seven Principles of Kwanzaa

UMOJA (oo-MOH-jah) Unity
To strive for and maintain unity in the family, community, nation, and race.

KUJICHAGULIA (koo-jee-chah-goo-LEE-ah) Self-determination
To define ourselves, name ourselves, create for ourselves, and speak for ourselves instead of being defined, named, created for, and spoken for by others.

UJIMA (oo-JEE-mah) Collective Work and Responsibility
To build and maintain our community together and make our sisters' and brothers' problems our problems and to solve them together.

UJAMAA (oo-jah-MAH-ah) Cooperative Economics
To build and maintain our own stores, shops, and other businesses and to profit from them together.

NIA (NEE-ah) Purpose
To make our collective vocation the building and developing of our community in order to restore our people to their traditional greatness.

KUUMBA (koo-OOM-bah) Creativity
To do always as much as we can, in the way we can, in order to leave our community more beautiful and beneficial than we inherited it.

IMANI (ee-MAH-nee) Faith
To believe with all our heart in our people, our parents, our teachers, our leaders, and the righteousness and victory of our struggle.

Maulana Karenga, *The African American Holiday of Kwanzaa: A Celebration of Family, Community and Culture* (Los Angeles: University of Sankore Press, 1989).